Lighten Up!

50 Jokes and Quotations

J o h n   S h a n n o n

 **Trafford** PUBLISHING®   **www.trafford.com**
North America & international
toll-free: 1 888 232 4444 (USA & Canada)
fax: 812 355 4082

Dedication

To my mother, Mary Ann Inez Shannon,

My mother died on my birthday in 2014, on April 2nd. She wished me a happy birthday in the morning before she died. I was turning 51 that day. I want to dedicate this book to her because she kept me alive. When I was six months old I got really bad pneumonia and I had 108-degree temperature. She wrapped me in cold compresses to keep me from going into convulsions so I would not develop epilepsy. And that was the time when I was in a coma for 21 days. I was intubated – they put a tube through my nose down into my left lung. And it collapsed my left lung, which is why I still have trouble with my left lung. It's my bad lung.

I want to dedicate this book to my mom because she loved me and she did a hell of a good job taking care of me. She quarantined me so I wouldn't get sick. She moved everything out of her bedroom and put me in there, and scrubbed it from top to bottom every day. She kept me from getting sick. She kept me alive. If it wasn't for her I wouldn't even be writing this book.

My mom's maiden name was Mary Ann Inez Gustafson; she was born on June 15, 1929. She had a Swedish background; my father was Irish and a touch of Scottish. My mother was really something. She was a good Christian woman. She believed in God and prayed to God to help get me better. And she not only prayed to God but she took care of me. She could have been a doctor if she had gone to school.

acknowledgements

Cover photo by Alexandra Miller.
Manuscript editing by Warren Djerf.

Jokes & Quotations

#*1)*

i take my meds only during the evening news:
5, 6, and 10.

#2)

When i lost my wisdom teeth, i also lost my wisdom.

#3)

i clean my plate with a clean-it butter and jelly sandwich.

#4)

i was born with one foot on the grave and the other on a banana peel.

#5)

Q: What day did the camel come to town?

a: Hump Day!

#6)

Knock Knock / Who's There?

Ya-Hoo / Ya-Hoo Who?

Ya-Hooooo!!!

#7)

Q: What type of letter do you write to walk out on your favorite deer tick?

A: A Deer Tick letter.

#*8)*

i will have a combo sandwich and a medium
cyanide.

#9)

Do not get crucified in the courtroom. You need experienced legal advice.

You need the law firm of Getcha, Gottam and Burnham.

#*10)*

Two gingerbread boys escaped from prison...
and i hear they're really tough cookies.

#*11)*

Q) What did the chronic asthmatic patient ask the octogenarian?

a) You got any oxygen?

#*12)*

Q) What do you do when you ride on a long bus ride?

a) You sit back and enjoy the obscenity.

#*13)*

Thank you blue-berry much.

#14)

i have hula-hooping cough.

#*15)*

Q)   What letter of the alphabet do you use
     when you're telling a lie?

a)   a-fib.

#*16)*

ed Zipper and the Trousers' had a hit song, "Oh no, my zipper's down."

#*17)*

The butcher introduced his wife: "Meet Patty."

#*18)*

Do not go deer hunting and save a few bucks.

#*19)*

At the Sh*t Creek Concession Stand, they have plenty of boats but they're all out of paddles.

#20)

What's Dracula's favorite Halloween food?
a Hallo-weiner.

#*21)*

Pay your bills now, for tomorrow the world comes to an end and we don't want to chase you all over hell!

#22)

Get a colonoscopy and look up the old address!

#23)

Why did the T-Rex go to the doctor? for a dino-sore.

#*24)*

i love to eat fruit Loops for breakfast, and that means i'm a cereal killer.

#25)

Lookie lookie, call to get some nookie.

#26)

What do you call it when the earth does a boogie-woogie? an earth quake.

#27)

Get insurance and get a piece of the rock upside your head.

#28)

We spend money the old fashioned way: we burn it!

#29)

God Bless america with applesauce.

#*30)*

Go to Colonoscopy Central, where we like to say, "Millions and millions of butts served."

#31)

Q) What three animals would you want in your home?

a) a tiger in bed, a Jaguar in the garage and a jackass to pay for it all.

#32)

Q)   How do you make holy water?

a)   You boil the hell out of it.

#33)

Q)   Why couldn't the pirate play cards?

a)   Because he was sitting on the deck.

#34)

Q) What kind of needle does an alien Seamstress use?

a) A Space needle.

#*35)*

i wonder why porcupines are not allowed in the petting zoo?

#*36)*

Q)   How do you fix a broken pumpkin?

a)   You put a patch on it.

#37)

Check the halls for boughs of holly.

#38)

i went to the doctor to find out what was wrong with my back. He said he didn't know, but he had a hunch.

#*39)*

Q) What's green and drills holes?

a) a drill pickle.

#*40)*

i thought i would try to work as a carpenter...but i got bored!

#41)

i went to a garage Sale and i bought a garage.
Now i got no place to put it.

#42)

Q) Why did they not allow elephants to be in the swimming pool?

a) Because they wouldn't keep their trunks up.

#*43)*

Q: What is it when a hypochondriac feels pain?

a) Champagne (Sham pain).

#44)

Hey diddle diddle, John jumped over the moon, John learned how to jump over the moon from ditching Jarrett. Editor's Note: Jarrett is man from John's past.

#*45)*

Q: What kind of pop does the Pope drink?

a) Pope-Si-Cola!

#46)

you take a waitress with a southern accent who says "i'm from Tulsa, Oklahoma, can i take your order?" and you say, "yes, i'll take the cole slaw please!"

#47)

if i die in Tennessee, Ship me back by C.O.D.

#*48)*

Q) Why shouldn't you look in the refrigerator on Thanksgiving?

a) Cuz the turkey's dressing?

#49)

My wife went into labor on Labor Day!

#50)

Here comes John Shannon, with all his Shenanigans!

#51)

Bonus Joke:

Once upon a time, there was a cat. and the cat died and went to the pearly gates of heaven, where he met St. Peter. St. Peter said, "you've been a good cat; i will let you into heaven. What do you wish for?" The cat said, "i wish for a nice comfy pillow to lay down and go to sleep on."

and then by and by, two mice died and went to heaven. at the pearly gates, St. Peter said, "you've been good mice. i will let you into heaven. What do you wish for?"

The mice said, "We would each like a pair of roller skates." And they got the roller skates.

The next day, St. Peter asked the cat, "How do you like heaven?" The cat said, "Oh i love heaven, and i love my pillow. And especially i loved the meals on wheels you sent me!"

John's Philosophy of Living – in His Own Words

My father taught me, and I live by this, that I am the captain of my own ship. I am responsible for where I take my ship. If I go off course and make a mistake, then I have to take full responsibility for my mistake and correct the situation. When I'm wrong I will try to correct it, because it takes guts to do that, to admit you're wrong.

There's all these talk about mass shootings today. I have never had a gun and I never will because I have enough smarts in my brain to negotiate with people. If I have a problem, I'll talk it out. That's what we all need to do. We all need to talk to each other and find out what's going on. The more we talk, the more we can heal. Guns are not the answer.

I don't believe in suicide either. I feel that killing yourself is the act of a coward. I have fought all my life to make something of myself and I have a lot to live for. If some people had to put up with all my mental and physical problems, they might resort to that. But no matter how bad my situation gets, I keep trying.

I like the song "Fight the Good Fight" by the band Triumph, released in 1981. That's a good song that describes me. Some of the lyrics are:

> *Don't get discouraged, don't be afraid, we can*
> *Make it through another day*
> *Make it worth the price we pay*
> *Keep up your spirit, keep up your faith, baby*
> *I am counting on you*
> *You know what you've got to do*
> *Fight the good fight every moment*
> *Every minute every day*

John Shannon lives in an assisted living facility in Brooklyn Center, Minnesota. As noted in the introduction, he's faced numerous health challenges since birth. Today he lives with a variety of health issues, both physical (like asthma and high blood pressure) and psychological (like schizophrenia). Despite these challenges, he strives to maintain a positive outlook in life, and maintaining his sense of humor is a prime way he does this. He likes to crack jokes, say funny sayings and make other interesting comments and observations that keep those around him laughing – and sometimes scratching their heads.

He enjoys music, playing bingo and watching science fiction shows, especially "Star Trek." He also uses his walker to perform personal-shopping services for other residents in his facility. Proceeds from sales of this book will help supplement his minimal government assistance income.

Printed in the United States
By Bookmasters